Original title:
Unsolved Mysteries of the Human Condition

Copyright © 2025 Creative Arts Management OÜ
All rights reserved.

Author: Franklin Stone
ISBN HARDBACK: 978-1-80566-060-6
ISBN PAPERBACK: 978-1-80566-355-3

The Perplexity of Choices

Should I have coffee or tea,
Do I want to climb a tree?
The menu has way too much,
I'll just order a light touch.

Should I wear red or blue,
Can't decide, don't have a clue.
I'll pick whatever's near,
Oops, I spilled my drink here!

The Weight of Invisible Chains

Why do I keep my old shoes,
They're full of holes, yet I refuse?
Like a dog chasing its own tail,
I'd trade them for a giant snail.

I step out with mismatched socks,
A fashion choice that surely rocks.
As I trip on my own feet,
My cat just thinks it's a treat.

The Dance of Fading Memories

Remember the time we lost the keys?
We searched for hours with such ease.
Finally found them in the fridge,
Next, we'll look for the lost bridge.

The stories fade, like a dream,
Once so loud, now a soft stream.
But laughter echoes in the air,
As we share our forgetful flair.

The Beauty in Brokenness

My phone cracked, but it still sings,
In life, strife can have its flings.
That flower pot that's tipped and cracked,
Holds memories of love we lacked.

The couch has springs that poke and prod,
Yet it holds dreams, like a warm facade.
Embrace the quirks, the goofy bends,
Life's odd charm is what transcends.

Shadows of an Empty Room

In the corner sits a chair, a ghostly seat,
Where dust bunnies gather for a dinner meet.
The fridge hums softly, a lullaby so sweet,
While shadows dance like they're in a comedy fleet.

An old sock flirts with a wobbly broom,
It claims it's off to join the sock puppet bloom.
While curtains twitch to watch the chaos loom,
A castle built in quiet — joy in the gloom.

The Illusion of Certainty

I once found solace in a cup of tea,
It said, "Life's full of answers, trust me, you'll see!"
But the sip was just hot air, oh woe is me,
Now I muse with my cat on who's got the key.

A fortune cookie promised I'd soon win a race,
So I ran in circles, oh what a disgrace!
The only thing I gained was a familiar face,
A neighbor who laughed and joined my strange chase.

Forgotten Songs of the Heart

The love notes I penned, forgotten by fate,
Slip through my fingers, sing a tune sedate.
They jive with the dust, oh what a first date!
A serenade lost in a birdcage gate.

A heart once so bold, now hums a shy tune,
It winks at the moon, as if to commune.
Dancing with echoes in a lonely saloon,
Where laughter is silent and hopes are marooned.

The Chilling Grip of Regret

Regret walks the dog, it barks with a frown,
It teases my choices as if they were clowns.
In the circus of life, I'm juggling my gown,
While acrobats tumble and the audience crowns.

A cup of spilled coffee drenches my cheer,
It's the pregnancy of thoughts I now hold dear.
Yet amidst the chaos, I laugh without fear,
For who wouldn't join in this raucous frontier?

The Puzzle of Being

Why do we all crave snacks so sweet?
Yet claim we seek the ultimate feat.
We ponder life in midnight chats,
While acting like we know the stats.

In search of truth, we wear disguises,
Pretending we're all wise and rises.
But when it comes to coffee spills,
Our genius fades with caffeine thrills.

With every choice we try to make,
We often stumble, hit a brake.
Like socks that vanish in the wash,
Our thoughts escape, a feathery squosh.

And in the end, we're not so clear,
While laughing hard through every fear.
We dance and prance, a silly spin,
Embracing fate with a cheeky grin.

Voices from the Abyss

The cider spills, a drippy mess,
We shout, 'It's fate!' then laugh, no stress.
The fridge door creaks, a ghostly sound,
All secrets hide, but laughter's found.

Nighttime whispers call me near,
They say my socks are full of cheer.
Yet echoes laugh in tones so sly,
While I pretend to dig and pry.

Why does my cat give knowing stares?
Is she the sage who truly cares?
She slinks away with a hint of sighs,
As I ponder under starry skies.

In shadows deep, the humor drips,
Like melting ice in tiny sips.
And through the giggles, wisdom breaks,
Life's oddities are all it takes.

Enigmas of a Wandering Mind

My thoughts like clouds get lost at sea,
Drifting past all reality.
With each strange twist, I find a joke,
Stumbling over a trivial poke.

The squirrel outside mimics my dread,
Chasing nuts, oh what a thread!
A simple life, oh so refined,
Yet deep inside, what's left behind?

Why do we laugh and then we pout?
So baffling—what's this all about?
A riddle wrapped in chocolate bars,
With each small laugh, we touch the stars.

The clock ticks loud, a comical race,
Each tick reminds me life's a chase.
So let's embrace the wild unknown,
And make each mystery feel like home.

The Weight of Unspoken Thoughts

In crowded rooms, we sip our brew,
With eyes that tell a million views.
The weight of silence fills the air,
As thoughts escape without a care.

Eyebrows raise in perfect sync,
Conversations weave, while none can think.
The jokes we share in muted tones,
Hide fascinating, funny bones.

Why do we fumble with our dreams?
While plotting joy with silly schemes.
Yet every pause brings laughter's ring,
As we dance under life's bright swing.

We laugh about the weight of words,
While watching pigeons chase their herds.
An unspoken truth we all can find,
Is joy rests lightly on every mind.

Fragments of an Unwritten Story

In a world of socks misplaced,
We ponder fate with a silly face.
What if cheese is really smart?
Will it reveal the cheeseboard's heart?

Naps that steal away our dreams,
But who decides the silly themes?
Is spaghetti a noodle's friend?
Or a twist with no start or end?

We search for clues in pizza crust,
And wonder why we all just must.
If fish could talk about their day,
Would they just swim, or swim away?

In every laugh, a riddle lies,
The secret life of French fries.
And if the sun wore shades so bright,
Would it accept a free delight?

Questions Between the Lines

Why do we hoard the items weird?
Like that old sock, what's it feared?
Do jellybeans have secret plots?
Or are they just for tying knots?

Is there a medal for the lost?
For every penny, what's the cost?
Why do we giggle at our phones?
Are they our friends or just old bones?

If clouds could dance upon the sky,
Would they join in our laugh or cry?
What dreams do puddles try to hold?
And do they shimmer just to be bold?

Could a cactus blush if it could?
Or would it stay stoic, staring good?
In every question that we ask,
Lies a truth we rarely grasp.

The Secrets We Carry

We carry dreams in pockets deep,
Along with crumbs we forgot to sweep.
What if our laughter had a voice?
Would it sing us a funny choice?

Each secret's like a ticklish spot,
Beware the jokes that we have got.
If chairs could share their daily gossip,
Would they wiggle with a little toss-up?

We hide our quirks beneath the page,
Like rodents plotting in a cage.
If tickles could set stories free,
Would they run off like a bumblebee?

In every dance, a tale unfurls,
With twirls of joy and silly whirls.
And if the moon could crack a grin,
Would it show us where it's been?

Labyrinths of the Soul

In labyrinths where laughter's lost,
What's the cost of the silly frost?
If our thoughts were tangled in a knot,
Would they shout, or just make a plot?

Why does our cat watch us so wise?
Is it plotting from those curious eyes?
If hiccups had a sense of pride,
Would they leap forth and run and hide?

Amidst the maze, where echoes dwell,
Do frozen smiles have a story to tell?
If umbrellas had a taste for rain,
Would they dance or just complain?

In every corner, humor peeks,
Disguised in whispers, laughter speaks.
And if we've wandered 'til we're old,
Would we find warmth in tales retold?

Embracing the Unknown

In a world full of quirks, we stumble and bumble,
Questions like jellybeans, we fumble and jumble.
The truth hides in corners, behind doors ajar,
Like a sock that you lost, still searching afar.

The coffee we spill leaves patterns on the floor,
Hints of life's chaos that we can't help but adore.
We laugh at the oddities, a dance with our fate,
Fools in a circus, it's never too late.

What's under the surface? A riddle, a joke?
Sometimes life's wisdom is wrapped up in smoke.
Chasing the shadows, we wear silly hats,
Finding the answers in giggles and spats.

So here's to the questions that tickle our minds,
To the playful adventures that curiosity finds.
With a wink and a grin, let's chase after glee,
Embracing the unknown, just you and me.

Threads of Time Unraveled

Time spins like a spider, with webs made of dreams,
The past likes to trip us, or so it seems.
A clock striking laughter, or was that a sneeze?
Dancing in circles, oh, what a tease!

We wear the old stories like mismatched socks,
Each one a reminder of life's crafty knocks.
The moments are fragile, like bubbles of soap,
Floating on whims, or the wildness of hope.

In the tapestry woven, odd patterns we find,
Like a shirt with a stain that has grown on your mind.
Threads of confusion all tangled and tied,
Bringing us chuckles as we slip and slide.

So let's toast to the hours, both silly and bright,
Navigating shadows, stepping into the light.
With laughter our compass, adventure our prime,
We'll unravel the secrets of this funny old time.

The Silence of Longing

In the quiet of night, when the moon starts to glow,
Whispers of wishes float gently and slow.
Oh, the things that we crave, like a donut at dawn,
A sweet kind of silence, a symphony drawn.

Longing for pizza when diets take hold,
Dreaming of ice cream, how bold and how cold!
Our hearts play the banjo, stringed with delight,
Wishing for answers that dance just out of sight.

We yearn for adventures, both big and quite small,
Like finding that one sock we lost in the hall.
The silence can giggle, can tickle, can tease,
Capturing moments, our souls left at ease.

So when craving a hug, or a slice of warm pie,
Know that the silence can make spirits fly.
In the stillness we find the hilarity's brew,
The silence of longing is giggles for two.

Faces in the Fog

Misty mornings greet with a veil and a grin,
Faces appear, disappear, let the games begin.
Is that my old neighbor or just a tall tree?
The fog loves to play, isn't it quite free?

Shadows are laughing, as they trip by the gate,
Whispers of secrets, with a wink and a fate.
Each face tells a story, but who could it be?
A ghost in a parka, or my Auntie Lee?

In the haze of confusion, we mingle and sway,
Every turn is a riddle, a cheeky ballet.
The fun in the fog is a whimsical place,
Where laughter and mischief share a warm embrace.

So next time you wander, don't fear what's unclear,
The faces may change, but the joy lingers near.
With each step we take, let's dance with the mist,
For the fog holds the laughter that we can't resist!

The Ink of Untold Stories

There's ink spilled on the pages, so bold,
Each tale waiting, reluctant to unfold.
A sock's missing—where does it go?
Does it dance in the light or put on a show?

The cat swears it's seen a ghost,
But really, it's just bread that's toast.
We scribble our tales, with giggles inserted,
While wise old trees stay mum, somewhat converted.

Oh, what secrets lie in kitchen drawers?
Do spoons hold grudges, or start trivial wars?
Life's a riddle, with punchlines so vague,
Like a jigsaw puzzle missing a leg.

So we laugh at life's quirks, its mystery fold,
In ink, we list stories yet to be told!

Tides of Unanswered Questions

The waves crash down with queries galore,
Why does the toaster burn bread, oh what a chore?
When the socks have a party, does the dryer just sigh?
And who let the cat know how to lie?

We ponder the snacks left alone on the shelf,
Does the chocolate know it must hide itself?
What lurks in the fridge on the bottommost shelf?
And do pickles dream of becoming themselves?

Why are there socks without proper mates?
Are they planning a scheme for colder states?
Life's like a joke where punchlines delay,
With laughter we follow the answers that stray.

So, ride the tides of laughter and jest,
For the questions we ask are perpetually blessed!

Across the Threshold of Understanding

Step right up to the great unknown,
Where reasoning's claimed as a shabby throne.
Can fish really fly, or is it a joke?
What are shadows, but the light's scared cloak?

We've crossed a threshold—it's wild and fun,
Did llamas invent shoes? Have we just begun?
Why do socks smell like a thousand year tale?
And who wrote the rules of the proverbial scale?

Questions arise, like bubbles afloat,
Do we float through dreamlands or just sit and gloat?
We trip on the truth with a gleeful grin,
In the maze of our minds, let the chaos begin!

So here we delve, in humor and cheer,
To dance on the edge of the things we hold dear!

The Veil of Collective Memory

Behind the veil of thoughts we share,
Did someone forget to comb their hair?
Was it Tuesday when this dance was a blast?
Or just a figment we thought would last?

Each memory twirls in its humorous spin,
Like a clown on a tricycle, it's bound to grin.
Do we all share tales of bizarre family quirks?
Or is it just me with those pajama smirks?

What's hidden behind the myths that we weave?
Can a rubber chicken help us believe?
In this tapestry, the laughter does flow,
Connecting our histories, stitched toe to toe.

So let's lift the veil, and share all the glee,
For our memories blend like a potpourri!

The Burden of Unsaid Goodbyes

In the café, I waved too late,
Now the pastry's on my plate.
I couldn't find my words to say,
So I just left them, blown away.

Scraps of courage on the floor,
Who knew leaving would mean more?
I dropped my coffee on my shoe,
Now my sock's a mess, who knew?

The laughter shared was bittersweet,
Did I trip over my own feet?
As I ponder what could have been,
My heart plays hide and seek again.

But in silence, I still believe,
There's joy in how we all perceive.
So here's to goodbyes yet unsaid,
I'll just laugh and make my bed.

Whispers in the Wind

The trees are gossiping again,
About how humans feel in rain.
They giggle 'bout love's funny dance,
While we shove our hearts in a can.

A breeze zips by with a sly grin,
"Told you not to chase the wind!"
But we just stand, our hair a mess,
As fate sprinkles down its jest.

Clouds above are like fluffy spies,
They watch our dreams, our awkward highs.
Do they laugh when we trip and fall?
Or are they waiting for a call?

So let's join the wind in its play,
Forget the rules, throw caution away.
In whispers, we'll share our silly grins,
With skies above, where laughter begins.

The Hall of Lost Dreams

In a hallway with doors ajar,
I found my hopes, not too bizarre.
One door led to a dancing cat,
Another had a talking hat.

A dream of flying, I forgot!
It's just a cloud in a parking lot.
Around the corner, a pizza slice,
Told me, "You're too nice, think twice!"

I stumbled on forgotten cheers,
Echoes of my childhood fears.
Why did I think I could win?
When dogs and cats both play to spin!

So here I sit, a dream collector,
In this strange hall of a great vector.
With laughs and sighs, I can't but grin,
Life's a puzzle, where to begin?

The Fragile Thread of Connection

Threads of laughter weave in air,
Like spaghetti, full of flair.
We tug and pull, and sometimes break,
Still mending all the bonds we make.

A coffee spill on an awkward date,
Leads to moments we celebrate.
A wink across the crowded room,
Who knew friendship could bloom?

In this web of silly ties,
We laugh at how we all disguise.
Each glance a knot, each smile a stitch,
In the fabric that makes us rich.

So let's dance on this tightrope tight,
With wobbling steps, we'll find our light.
In the fragile threads we create,
There lurks a joy to celebrate!

The Enigma of Change

One day I woke with hair of green,
My socks mismatched, a sight unseen.
What happened to the plans I made?
They vanished like the sunlight's fade.

The bus that never came today,
The cat that tried to join the fray.
Life's puzzles jostle, twist and twine,
I laugh and cry while sipping wine.

With every turn, the truth will bend,
A riddle wrapped in my best friend.
Did I gain wisdom? Maybe so,
Just wish my plants would learn to grow.

In circles round, we dance and spin,
The questions linger deep within.
While change parades in silly hats,
I chase my thoughts like cheeky cats.

Reflections in a Shattered Glass

Mirror, mirror, cracked and loud,
You show my face beneath a shroud.
Who's that stranger grinning wide?
Maybe it's the snacks I've tried.

The world shows me a skewed design,
Like pizza dough but without the pine.
Oh, how I wish for clarity,
Instead, I see my own disparity.

Each shard reflects a different me,
A goofy grin, a cringe, oh glee!
In chaos lies a certain charm,
That adds a little extra harm.

Behind the glass, a joke unfolds,
As laughter mingles with the bold.
Oh, shattered dreams can still be fun,
Just paint them bright and watch them run.

Secrets Lurking in the Shadows

In corners dark, where secrets creep,
A lamp's light flickers, but I can't sleep.
What's that noise? A sock? A shoe?
Or maybe just the ghosts of stew?

They whisper tales of lost romance,
Of mismatched socks and epic pants.
A shadow darts, oh what a fright,
Did it steal my sandwich last night?

With every creak, a secret shared,
Like hiding from a truth impaired.
Is it the cat or just my snack?
Oh life, you're such a funny hack.

In shadows dance the quirks of fate,
A laughter bubble, can't wait, can't wait.
So here's to all the weird and wise,
Let's toast our quirks beneath the skies.

The Language of Lost Hope

Hope gave a speech, but lost its rhyme,
It stumbled on the path of time.
With twisty words and silly phrases,
It tripped on dreams, lost in mazes.

Each day I try to speak it clear,
But hope just giggles, draws me near.
It says, 'Just dance, forget the fuss!'
And echoes back, 'It's all a plus!'

In every sigh, a chuckle hides,
Hope wears a cloak of fumbles, glides.
It whispers sweetly, breaks a rule,
'The greatest jest is life's own school.'

So if you feel that hope is gone,
Just check your socks, they might be drawn.
A wink, a smile, embrace the plight,
For laughter makes the dark seem bright.

In Search of What Lies Beneath

Every closet has its ghostly cheer,
To hide the socks we've held so dear.
With dust bunnies grinning in the light,
They whisper secrets, oh what a sight.

The fridge hums softly, a chilly friend,
Where leftover lasagna dreams of its end.
We dive in deep, with forks in hand,
Searching for treasures in a takeout land.

In the attic, old memories fade,
In the shadows, a pirate parlay is made.
With cardboard swords and pirate hats,
We sail with cats, oh how they spat!

Yet what lies beneath, we cannot claim,
Just jumbled stories lost in the game.
Laughing at life's peculiar quirks,
In the deep end, that's where humor lurks.

The Masks We Wear

Behind every grin, a story hides,
A clown's big nose speaks of wild rides.
With glitter and paint, we dance through glee,
While crumbs of chaos cling, cannot see.

In rush-hour traffic, we polish our glare,
Each fender-bender, a performer's scare.
As we beep our horns in perfect time,
It's a ballet of anger, oh what a rhyme.

When we meet at parties, a laugh we trade,
With friendly waves beneath the charade.
Yet deep inside, we jest and fret,
What is real? We puzzle, we sweat.

So, pop on your mask, let's join the charade,
In this theater of life, we've each made our grade.
With a bow and a wink, we slip on the air,
For beneath all the laughter, we're simply laid bare.

Beneath the Surface of Serenity

Waves crash softly, the beach is a joke,
While seagulls swoop down, a mischievous folk.
Beneath the calm, a cacophony plays,
Shells hide their secrets in sun-drenched bays.

On the yoga mat, we find our peace,
Pretzel poses that bring us release.
But deep in the mind, a squirrel on a spree,
Chasing thoughts like nuts, jump oh so free.

In the garden, tranquility waits,
But bees and ants argue over the gates.
A ladybug sneezes and sets off a chase,
The battle of bloom, no winning grace.

So whirl in the dance of this serene charade,
With giggles and wiggles, let worries cascade.
For laughter will echo above and below,
In a world where the seeds of humor do grow.

Reflections of a Fleeting Thought

Once I had wisdom, a great shining star,
But it slipped through my fingers, oh how bizarre.
In the shower, great ideas bubble and pop,
Yet when I step out, they simply just drop.

At coffee breaks, I brew my best schemes,
But logic makes faces, shattering dreams.
With frothy milk mustaches, we sip and we sigh,
Missing the answers, we shrug and we cry.

Life's a riddle, wrapped in a grin,
With puzzles of fate, where laughter must win.
So chase the faint echoes of whims and wits,
For clarity hides in the jester's tricks.

In fleeting reflections, we dance on the floor,
With thoughts like balloons that float out the door.
In the end, dear friend, we laugh and we play,
For each fleeting thought makes the dull fade away.

Dreams That Slip Away

I chased a cloud with candy shoes,
While dancing with a purple moose.
The clock ticked loud, I raised my gaze,
But dreams dissolved in silly ways.

I painted rainbows on my toast,
And sang a tune from coast to coast.
But time, that sneaky little brat,
Just swiped my dream and left me flat.

I wrote a speech for peacock's pride,
But he just laughed and turned aside.
I searched for wishes in the dark,
As fish and frogs began to bark.

So here I sit with dreams of pie,
And wishful thoughts that make me sigh.
For laughter's all that I can take,
As dreams, they slip like cheese from cake.

Fragments of a Broken Mirror

In shards of glass, my smile reflects,
A world of laughter and projects.
I see my nose is slightly bent,
And wonder if my hair's well-spent.

The mirror laughs, a jester's glare,
It shows my socks, a silly pair.
I wave goodbye to wisdom's stare,
And greet the chaos in my hair.

Each piece reveals a funky dance,
As wisdom trips in silly pants.
An eye for style, a hand for cheer,
Within the cracks, my dreams appear.

So here's to flaws that give us glee,
In broken glass, I can't help but see,
That laughter sparkles where it's bright,
In fragments caught by morning light.

The Language of Unseen Pain

My heart speaks loud in whispers soft,
When busy bees take off aloft.
They buzz about, my thoughts collide,
And light a flame I cannot hide.

I trip on words, they play their tricks,
Like jumping beans on pogo sticks.
The silence laughs at what I say,
While pizza dreams just float away.

I wear my heart as shirt of loud,
A polka-dot that screams, "I'm proud!"
Though pain may play its subtle tune,
I'll dance with squirrels under the moon.

So here's to joy when things go wrong,
In quirky tales that help us along.
For hidden hurts may twist and sway,
But laughter brings the light of day.

Unknown Desires

I crave a shoe that's made of cheese,
Or maybe socks that dance with ease.
A fridge that sings and makes me toast,
And wears a hat like silly ghosts.

My heart desires a car of ice,
That drips and dribbles, oh so nice.
It drives me round the wacky bend,
While lending me a paper friend.

I long for clouds that taste like pie,
And fruits that float, oh my, oh my!
The laughter bubbles from the skies,
As wishes dance before my eyes.

So let me dream these giggly dreams,
Of chocolate rivers and silly beams.
In unknown wants, I find the fun,
As life's a game, I've just begun.

Enigmatic Encounters

Four socks vanish without a clue,
Are they plotting? Who knew!
Laughing at our silly plight,
Dancing away into the night.

Do spare keys hold secret powers?
Or just make us search for hours?
As we ponder and debate,
They giggle, hiding from our fate.

In cupboards, lives a cheeky ghost,
Who finds our leftovers the most.
With a shout and slight dismay,
He devours our snacks and runs away!

What makes us crave absurd delight?
Like wearing shoes on the wrong foot tight.
A shoestring theory yet unproven,
In this world of chaos, we're still movin'.

The Curiosity of Hidden Tears

Why do onions make us cry so loud?
Are they setting up their own proud crowd?
With each chop, an enigmatic laugh,
Wishing for a teary photograph.

Worry peeks from behind the door,
While laughter trips on the kitchen floor.
We hide our frowns beneath the glee,
Telling secrets to a cup of tea.

Why are socks unmatched in every heap?
They conspire while we're fast asleep.
Under the bed, secrets recline,
Mysteries dance in laundry divine.

Jokes forgotten in a fleeting hour,
Why's the fridge light brighter than a flower?
Unanswered quirks and smiles we'll keep,
Let's embrace the joy in our sweeping leap.

The Chasm of Yearning

A slice of cake no one can find,
Lies in the chasm of the mind.
A longing look for forgotten sweet,
What we crave is a laugh on repeat.

Every puzzle piece feels a tad askew,
Like that one sock, it's never a two.
Yet in our hearts, we play our part,
Crafting giggles in the art.

The wish for socks to find their mate,
Like our dreams, they congregate.
In places dark, yet brightly lit,
A yearning here to never quit!

Between the what-ifs and the memes,
Our lives are stitched with glowing seams.
So let's spin yarns and shed the stress,
In absurdity, we find our best!

When Time Stands Still

Why does coffee drip at its own pace?
Like it's caught in a slow-motion race?
Muffin tops are the envy of all,
While life's mysteries down the hall.

The clock ticks loudly, then shifts to sigh,
As we ponder the cheese pie up high.
Each minute feels like a wayward cat,
Curled up cozy; imagine that!

Do we grasp moments, or do they elude?
Is time a trickster, a lyricist rude?
With the chaos we'll always adjust,
In randomness, there's gleeful trust.

So let us smile at the passing hours,
In our time warp, we find the powers.
Each tick and tock we giggle at,
This game of life—imagine that!

Dances with the Unfathomable

Why do socks vanish in the wash?
Can they really dance, or just swash?
We search for answers, true or fake,
While piña coladas melt in the lake.

The cat knows secrets we can't understand,
Plotting and scheming, just like a band.
It twirls on the counter, claims the spotlight,
While we chuckle and say, "What a sight!"

We ponder life's quirks over a pie,
As no one can guess the reason why.
Grumpy old ghosts play peekaboo,
Leaving us baffled, what can we do?

With wild tales spun from a grandma's mouth,
The truth sways north, while the lies go south.
In every twist, we laugh till we cry,
Whatever the reason, oh my, oh my!

Labors of the Heart's Query

Why do we trip on our own two feet?
Logic takes breaks, that's just our beat.
We chase after love like a dog with a shoe,
Sniffing for answers, just me and you.

Some say it's chocolate, others a smile,
But seeking sweet love can take a while.
We write out our feelings, then toss 'em away,
Forget how to flirt—'Is it Tuesday today?'

Our hearts are puzzles with missing pieces,
Yet every sweet failure, laughter increases.
We fall for the wrong ones, like rain in the sun,
But let's face it: heartbreak is half the fun.

So grab your heart's map and let's make a plan,
To dance with delight, an odd little clan.
We'll stumble through life, chasing what's true,
With love as our mischief, just me and you!

Between the Choices of Now and Then

Should I wear polka dots or stripes today?
Life's fashion runway is quite the ballet.
The fridge is a mystery, food's out to get,
When hunger strikes, our minds are a fret.

We ponder our futures with coffee in hand,
Should I join a circus or travel to land?
While dreams of adventure waltz in our heads,
The couch whispers softly, "Stay here instead."

The clock ticks loudly but time feels so thin,
We plan for the moment, yet always lose spin.
Stuck between choices like socks in a wash,
We whirl around fancifully—not a quash!

So laugh as you wobble, enjoy the sweet strife,
Embrace every choice, it's all part of life.
When asked why you dance, say, "Oh, just because,"
Between now and then, look for the buzz!

Notes from the Edge of Reason

At the edge of reason, confusion takes flight,
Worries get tangled, just hold on tight.
The laundry's a beast, the dishes a chore,
While I ponder why it's fun to explore.

We laugh at the chaos of life on a whim,
As logic runs circles, it's looking quite grim.
Why chase after answers like ducks on a pond?
Embrace the absurd, it's really a bond.

The fridge, a portal to snacks of pure bliss,
Whispers sweet secrets—oh, don't you dare miss!
Does it truly matter if we're wrong or right?
As long as we're here, let's dance through the night.

So tiptoe on questions and giggle with glee,
For reason's a puzzle, and we hold the key.
Let's scribble our thoughts, both silly and bold,
In notes from the edge, let the fun unfold!

The Search for Meaning in Chaos

In the middle of a mess, we search so keen,
Like finding socks in a dryer, they're nowhere seen.
Laughing at the snippets of sense we can find,
As our thoughts bounce about, a carnival blind.

Clowns in our minds, juggling logic with flair,
Each theory a balloon that floats in the air.
We chase them with nets made of hope and of dreams,
While reality answers with giggles and screams.

Beneath the Stars, We Wander

Under the cosmos, we trip and we glide,
Stumbling on wonders, like puppies who slide.
Searching for answers written in star dust,
With each fallen comet, we hoot and we trust.

Aliens grinning, they point and they mock,
'Your questions are goofy, like socks on a clock.'
Yet, in their strange humor, there lies some delight,
As we dance among galaxies, lost in the night.

The Silence Between Heartbeats

In the pauses of life, where no sound exists,
We ponder our purpose as if we're on lists.
A heartbeat that whispers, 'What's all this for?'
While multiplying snacks at the local snores.

Time ticks away, we laugh in between,
Those moments of stillness, awkward but keen.
Tickle the silence, it giggles absurd,
In quiet, odd laughter, our truths are inferred.

Footprints in an Untrodden Path

On a path less traveled, our footprints confuse,
Like mismatched shoes at a dance with no clues.
Do we follow the footprints or make our own way,
As we trip over hopes that we tossed in the fray?

Each step's a giggle, a slip on our part,
The compass of laughter is our guiding chart.
In the woods of our doubts, we stumble and spin,
But in joy, we find paths where the fun can begin.

The Echoes of Silent Hearts

In the corner of the bar, they laugh,
Hidden tales, a comic gaffe.
Hearts that whisper, not quite loud,
Fumbling secrets in front of the crowd.

A wink, a nod, a gaze so shy,
Pancakes for love, oh me, oh my!
Silent serenades under the moon,
As pigeons plot their comical swoon.

They dance with shadows, feet askew,
Chasing tropes, just a motley crew.
Misdirected glances, a tango gone wrong,
Life's a jest in this funny song.

In the chaos of heartbeats, joy takes flight,
As we laugh at the dark, turning wrongs to right.
So raise a toast to the hues we wear,
Echoes of laughter fill the midnight air.

Secrets Beneath the Skin

Underneath the laughter, a tickle of truth,
A bellyache built from the lies of youth.
Jokes about troubles that fester and grow,
Dancing around, a humorous show.

What's that itch? A story untold,
A missing sock, the fate of the bold.
Scratch the surface, hear the giggle,
Truth hides in shadows, just trying to wiggle.

With every blush comes a playful grin,
Scratching for answers where we begin.
Tickle my fancy with tales of the surreal,
Underneath, oh my, what's the deal?

So peel back a layer, just one more spin,
Unwrap the fun hiding deep within.
Beneath our masks, in silence we hide,
Silly truths laughing together inside.

Veils of Illusion

Behind every curtain, a puppet on strings,
Twirling in circles, oh what crazy things!
Life's a facade, who wears it best?
A daily drama, a comic jest.

Laughter as armor, we wade through the show,
Slipping on banana peels, here we go!
With every misstep, a chuckle is born,
In the play of existence, we're all a bit worn.

Mismatched socks in a dance of despair,
Trying to balance, but who really cares?
Each veil we lift shows a jest behind,
Where humor resides, and life redefined.

A hurricane of smiles in the chaos we weave,
Unraveling threads in the moments we grieve.
So raise your glass, let the laughter swell,
In the grand illusion, we all know too well.

Unwritten Pages of Existence

Blank sheets of paper, what to inscribe?
Writing our laughs with a whimsical vibe.
Each stroke a giggle, each scribble a cheer,
Dancing with uncertainty, banishing fear.

A footprint in sand, washed by a wave,
A punchline forgotten, the joker's brave.
Piecing together this riddle of life,
Joking through chaos, amidst all the strife.

The ink may run dry, but still we compose,
Filling in blanks as the humor bestows.
Imagine the tales in the margins unwritten,
A canvas of chuckles, by laughter we're smitten.

So here's to the moments, unwritten and wild,
The funny absurdity, like thoughts of a child.
In the book of our journey, let joy take the stage,
As we fill every line on this unwritten page.

Echoes of the Unseen

In shadows where the laughter hides,
Whispers dance on silly tides.
Mysterious socks lost in the wash,
Perhaps they went to a sock-bash, posh!

With every giggle, echoes swell,
What stories do the curtains tell?
A ghost with a penchant for pranks,
Stealing snacks and doing dank flanks!

The bathroom light flickers and fades,
Did that toilet brush just throw shades?
Each creak of the wood is a playful tease,
Could it be ghosts enjoying a breeze?

We ponder the weight of shadows unseen,
Did they catch a glimpse of our dreams?
In corners, they chuckle at our plight,
Blessing our blunders under the night!

The Elusive Nature of Time

Tick-tock goes the clock on the wall,
Why does it think it knows it all?
Minutes stretch like elastic bands,
While snacks are devoured in wild bands!

Lunch turns to dinner in a blink of an eye,
Wasn't it just breakfast, oh my, oh my!
Time plays tricks, like the cat with a yarn,
Each unravel leads to an unplanned charm.

Old photos whisper tales from the past,
Carried in frames, they dance and laugh fast.
Do they bend time or twist around?
Or just get lost in memories sound?

While calendars mock, we'll eat cake galore,
Each slice holds secrets of down-to-the-core.
So let cheers echo through the halls,
For time is a party that never stalls!

The Threads That Connect Us

Invisible strings weave the air,
Binding us close with laughter to share.
A wink here, a nudge there,
Silly bonds dance without a care.

The neighbor's cat thinks he's in charge,
Stealing attention, living large.
While we bicker over who's the best,
The cat just yawns and takes a rest.

Shared jokes ripple, a thread pulls tight,
Creating a tapestry, pure delight.
In mishaps of life, we gracefully fall,
Like spaghetti flung against the wall!

So let's stitch laughter in every seam,
For together, we're more than we seem.
In the fabric of life, joy's a must,
Hold on tight, together we trust!

Wanderings of a Restless Spirit

A specter floats on a pogo stick,
Bouncing around with candor so slick.
It steals all the cookies from the tin,
Leaving crumbs for giggles, where to begin?

Haunted houses have the best of times,
Chasing after shadows in silly rhymes.
They tickle the fancies of who walks by,
Do they giggle, or just flutter and fly?

Late-night whispers under blankets and sheets,
Who knew ghosts could dance to our beats?
With every creak, they twirl in delight,
For every soul has a wild night!

So raise a glass to the wanderers bold,
Life is a riddle, a story retold.
In wanderings, laughter's the best delight,
Join the dance in the shimmering night!

An Odyssey of Shadows

In search of socks that wander free,
I find their trail in mystery.
Did they escape on a daring quest?
Or hide away, just needing rest?

My lunchbox whispers tales of yore,
Of sandwiches and snacks galore.
Yet each adventure comes with a price,
A soggy bread, oh, isn't that nice?

In corners dark, where dust bunnies play,
Lurks the truth of yesterday.
Do they conspire to steal my snacks?
Or run a school for misfit wax?

A distant laugh from the depths of my mind,
Reminds me I'm both lost and kind.
Where do I go if night falls fast?
I'll follow shadows, for a laugh, at last!

The Ghosts of Choices Not Made

In the fridge lies a pizza slice,
Reminders of the night, quite nice.
But what of the salad, so brave and green?
Who chose this path, so rarely seen?

Did I pick Netflix or a good book?
My couch can tell; it gives me a look.
The popcorn's gone, with secrets to tell,
Of binge-watching nights, oh, we had so well.

Each fork in the road, I ponder and laugh,
Do I roam the wilds or take my bath?
The ghosts of my choices haunt my floor,
They moan for the salsa and chips I ignore.

Yet here I stand, with options galore,
In a world that opens a million doors.
What if I choose to dance with the cat?
A wild turn, oh how about that?

Whispers of a Fading Past

In grandma's attic, a trunk sits tight,
Filled with the memories of lost delight.
A broken watch, a musty hat,
What stories reside in that old welcome mat?

Dust motes twirl in a sunlit beam,
Reflecting fragments of a forgotten dream.
A typewriter keys still dance and sing,
Did it once create the next big thing?

Old photos peek through a veil of gray,
With smiles so bright, they seem to say:
'We danced on tables and sang to the stars,
But where's that charm? It's lost in the jars!'

As memories fade like whispers of air,
I chuckle at ghosts who once filled the chair.
Each trinket a portal, each laugh a spell,
Did we age or just learn how to rebel?

Echoes of the Unsung

In the bathroom's mirror, I stand so bold,
Reflecting stories yet to be told.
An opera of shampoo, a duet of soap,
In the realm of the bathroom, I'm the pope!

Socks and sandals, a fashion faux pas,
In the land of style, it's just a big flaw.
Yet echoes of laughter, they float in the air,
As I navigate life with questionable care.

The dog looks on, a critic of sorts,
While I engage in my bathrobe retorts.
With a rubber duck choir, we'll sing out loud,
To the tune of misfits, we're wacky and proud!

In outlandish gait, I dance through the hall,
What's next, I ponder, as I trip and fall.
Life's a grand circus, with clowns at the front,
And I'm just the jester, enjoying the hunt!

Fables of the Human Heart

In a world where socks go missing,
And sandwiches seem to vanish,
We ponder life's odd little puzzles,
Hungry for answers that don't quite banish.

Cats rule the roost with a flick of a tail,
While we chase our tails in a frantic hail,
Love letters are lost, but memes take their place,
In the race of romance, we all give chase.

The fridge hums secrets of dinners gone cold,
While we sift through dreams that refuse to unfold,
Friendship's a dance with two left feet,
Yet somehow we twirl to a quirky beat.

And in the end, as the sun sinks low,
Perhaps the joke's on us, don't you know?
We're all just fables of a whimsical art,
Eternally searching for whence we start.

The Enigma of Everyday Existence

Why is it that coffee spills at dawn?
Like life's little riddle, just somewhat drawn,
Each mug a canvas, a drip or two,
Creating chaos in morning's view.

We pretend to be mature with a well-placed tie,
But inside we're all just kids wanting to fly,
Finding joy in the simple, the slightly absurd,
Like dancing in rain, it's the unsung word.

An inbox full of emails, so urgent and dire,
Yet Netflix whispers, "Just one more fire!"
The tug of the couch against daily grind,
Laughter is key when the mind feels confined.

So toast to the moments wrapped in delight,
The enigmas of living, both silly and bright,
For life's greatest questions may puzzle and tease,
Yet we soak in the laughter, a sweet little tease.

Masks and Mirrors

In the mirror, a stranger with wild hair stares,
He's trying to be meaningful, but life's full of flares,
With each mask we don, we play our own roles,
A comedy show in which everyone strolls.

Behind every smile hides a tale that's grand,
Of unexpected hiccups and plans unplanned,
We juggle our dreams like clowns in a tent,
Fumbling through life, just a tad discontent.

The mirror reflects what we choose to reveal,
A wink or a grin, a quickened appeal,
Yet beneath all the laughter and grand flourish,
Lie whispers of worries that dare to nourish.

So let's don our masks with a wink and a twirl,
For life's a big stage, let the confetti unfurl,
With humor in hand, we'll dance through the night,
In this theatre of life, we're all seeking light.

In Search of the Lost Connections

Where did that phone charger vanish away?
A mystery of life we face every day,
In search of the freedom from dead battery blues,
We wrangle our devices, avoiding the snooze.

Friends send their greetings, lost in the Void,
Text messages linger where joy's been destroyed,
In the digital age, what's connection, you ask?
It's emojis and memes disguised as a mask.

But somewhere between selfies and swipes on the phone,
We crave that laughter in voices we know,
Laughter's a signal that transcends time and space,
It binds us together and brightens the place.

So let's raise a glass to the friends lost in gaps,
And find them again through each old-school clap,
In search of the echoes of giggles and cheer,
For in every connection, we hold life dear.

The Dichotomy of Existence

Life's a dance of joy and woe,
Like a jester in a vibrant show.
We laugh at fate's absurd decree,
As socks vanish in laundry glee.

A bridge between the bright and bleak,
In every clown, there's wisdom's peek.
We chase the cheese, the fickle goal,
While yearning still for half a roll.

In shadows, smiles take curious forms,
Nonsensical in life's crazy norms.
A sandwich talks, a chair does prance,
Oh, the wonder of this wild dance!

In paradox, our truth we find,
With giggles soft, our fate aligned.
We ponder deep, yet all the while,
Life's just a riddle wrapped in style.

Whispers of an Abandoned Path

Once a road, now overgrown,
With gnome-sized signs, I roam alone.
The trees gossip secrets untold,
Of squirrels and magic, brave and bold.

A broken compass plays its prank,
Sending me off toward the plank.
I stroll where lost boots gather dust,
And giggle at the woodland rust.

The moon chuckles in sheer delight,
As shadows dance with spirits at night.
Each turn reveals a quirky friend,
A turtle who pretends to blend.

My path may stray, yet here I grin,
With oddities and tales within.
Though maps may fail and roads go blind,
In laughter's echo, joy I find.

The Art of Unraveling

Life's yarn tangled in a ball,
Each pull reveals a funny fall.
Knots of wisdom, twists of fate,
A cat declines to contemplate.

With fingers crossed, I tug and tease,
Unravel truths as soft as cheese.
A sweater knits my ponderings wide,
While laughter weaves through every side.

In every stitch, a story grows,
Of missed connections and clownish prose.
I drop the needle, dance a jig,
And toast the tales, both big and fig.

When threads collide, what joy ignites,
In the art of life, oh, what delights!
So pluck those strings and sing your song,
For in the chaos, we belong.

The Sorrow of Forgotten Faces

In every crowd, a face once known,
Lost in the shuffle, all alone.
We smile at strangers in a sea,
Yet ghosts of jesters sway and flee.

A wink was missed, a laugh forgot,
While juggling life, our minds are caught.
Oh, where did all the good times go?
In unseen corners, shadows grow.

With every blink, a memory fades,
Of silly hats and joyous parades.
We raise a toast to those unseen,
As laughter echoes—mirthy, keen.

In nostalgia's grip, we find our place,
With echoes of the silly face.
Though time may steal our former glee,
We won't forget how fun it can be.

Beyond the Horizon of Certainty

We wear our hats so tilted,
Question marks, not quite spilt.
Chasing shadows, we all dance,
While plants debate, they take a chance.

The moon mocks us with a grin,
As we ponder where we've been.
Socks on hands, it's quite the trend,
Do they make sense? It bends, it bends!

Logic leaves, it takes a flight,
Cats do yoga in full sight.
We eat the cake, and then we sigh,
As crumbs of truth just pass us by.

Questions stirring like a stew,
Who mixed the blue with all that glue?
A parrot cheers, it knows the game,
As reality just calls our name.

The Uncharted Pathways of Self.

In the mirror, a grin too wide,
Is that me? I want to hide.
Juggling dreams like oranges bright,
While socks have fights without a fight.

I wonder if my coffee knows,
The secrets no one ever shows.
With every sip, a tale unfolds,
Of time-traveling, donut-holding golds.

Life's a series of mismatched socks,
With wisdom hidden in the clocks.
Dancing pigeons, they have a say,
As I trip on thoughts that stray.

Sprinklers splash, a cosmic joke,
In a world that's made of smoke.
We giggle at what's left untried,
With laughter echoing inside.

Whispers in the Dark

In the night, the shadows chat,
About the mouse that wears a hat.
Bouncing ideas, they seem so grand,
Should we build a castle made of sand?

Echoes giggle in the moon's light,
Can dreams take flight? Oh, what a sight!
Invisible friends, with tales to weave,
Should we trust what we believe?

With every creak, a story stirs,
As the floor dances, who prefers?
A giggle here, a sigh over there,
What was it all? Just tales we share.

Whispers, whispers, oh so sly,
The cat just winked, oh my, oh my!
With every giggle, wisdom's a lark,
As we wander through the dark.

Shadows of Forgotten Dreams

Dreams play hide and seek, so sly,
In the garden of thoughts, they fly.
Kites in a breeze of ice cream hopes,
We search for them with colorful ropes.

The fish in the stream told a joke,
About a sad hat that couldn't poke.
Flip-flops tango with paper boats,
While spaghetti twirls in need of coats.

We tiptoe through the whispers of past,
Chasing shadows, when will they last?
With every twinkle, a riddle cheer,
What's lost might be drawing near.

Frogs wear crowns, and they all croak,
The punchline waits, can we invoke?
In laughter's light, we find our way,
Where forgotten dreams like to play.

Whispers in the Void

In the closet, socks conspire,
To escape the laundry's ire.
Why do keys play hide and seek?
Is it magic, or just a leak?

We ponder life's odd little cues,
Like why we never trust our shoes.
The cereal talks, a clumsy bowl,
Whispers secrets to the soul.

What makes a cat so utterly sly?
While dogs just fetch and never lie.
The fridge hums a lullaby,
What's it hiding? We often sigh.

In shadows cast by morning light,
We dance to tunes that feel just right.
A riddle wrapped in a snack,
Unravel it, or just sit back.

Shadows of Forgotten Dreams

In the attic, old hats reside,
Once worn with flair, now full of pride.
What dreams did they once convey?
With each dusty twirl, they sway.

A toaster pops with a loud cheer,
"Your breakfast's ready, my dear!"
Yet burnt edges tell a tale,
Of moments lost, a morning fail.

The remote is lost, nobody cares,
Under cushions, it stealthily stares.
A quest for a show, never too late,
Our binge-watching cannot wait.

While shadows dance on the cracked wall,
We laugh at ghosts who can't recall.
What makes us chuckle at the unseen?
Perhaps it's all just in our dream.

Echoes of the Unseen

Echoes reverberate on a Tuesday night,
A sock puppet's laughter fills the light.
What stories do the walls confide?
With splatters of paint, the chaos can't hide.

The fridge whispers, "Let me cool your tale,"
A diet's promise, doomed to fail.
Yet here we munch, a snack parade,
In the realm of odd decisions made.

Tick-tock goes the clock, oh so sly,
A reminder that time can just fly.
Why do we trip over shoes and dreams?
It seems life's silliness reigns, or so it seems.

In echoes loud of laughter bright,
We chase shadows 'til the dawn's first light.
The oddities of life paint a smile,
With moments that stay for just a while.

The Light Beneath the Surface

Beneath the couch, the remote waits,
A guardian of our binge-watching fates.
Why must laundry always reappear?
As socks conspire, ever so near.

A cat meows a philosophical tune,
Under the sun, lazy as a loon.
Why do we fear the unknown parts?
When mystery lingers in all our hearts?

The plants whisper secrets of sunlit days,
As we dance through life in curious ways.
What makes the toast land butter-side down?
It's such a riddle at times that we frown.

With light that twinkles through the blue,
We laugh at chaos, it's nothing new.
For in the shadows and laughter bright,
We find our truths, often a delight.

Dance of the Unbeknownst

In the haze of a party, an owl wears a hat,
Bopping to the rhythm, so clever and fat.
Spectacles askew, he snorts with delight,
While humans just wonder, who turned off the light?

A cat on the dance floor, with moves quite absurd,
Practices his moonwalk, he's never deterred.
Birds critique from the rafters, sipping their tea,
As the owl starts a conga, daring them to flee.

The cheese on the table, now shakes with a song,
It wobbles and jiggles, joins in with the throng.
Humans all giggle, forgetting their woes,
As shadows lend voices to this strange tableau.

So come, dance along with the quirks of the night,
Where nonsense reigns loudly and wrong feels just right.
We twirl on the edge of what we can't see,
In a world full of questions, just follow the glee.

Beneath the Surface of Perception

A goldfish in glasses, he squints at the sky,
"Are clouds made of candy? Please tell me, oh my!"
His bowl is a fortress, his castle is grand,
Yet he dreams of the ocean, a faraway land.

A squirrel with a cookie seeks wisdom in trees,
While thinking that life is a soft summer breeze.
He sprawls on a branch, contemplating his fate,
"Why shout at the postman? It's never too late!"

Two ants bartering crumbs, they whisper with flair,
"What's better than sugar? A world full of air!"
They plot their next venture, a picnic that's bold,
While squirrels debate, who has the best hold.

So slice through the layers, enjoy every show,
In a universe swirling with laughter and woe.
Look closer, oh friend, 'neath the surface you tread,
Where answers are silly and fun spins your head.

Chasing Fleeting Shadows

On a sunlit lawn, two shadows take flight,
One's chasing the other, it's quite a wild sight.
"Catch me if you can!" cries the brave little shade,
While the grass giggles softly, secure in its glade.

A dog joins the dancing, all paws and great cheer,
Barking at shadows that flicker so near.
Each time he leaps forward, they dart out of reach,
His antics provoke a philosophical speech.

What are we really, but figures in time?
A jest at existence, a peculiar mime.
With every small prance, they ponder their fate,
As the sun plays a trick, oh, isn't it great?

So waltz with those shadows, let humor prevail,
In the chase of our lives, where laughter won't fail.
What's lost in the twilight, we'll never unearth,
But oh, how we dance, in this curious birth.

When Twilight Holds Its Breath

A cat with a monocle sips tea in the dusk,
And debates with a mouse, "Should I wear a tux?"
With dignified fur, they swap witty remarks,
As night settles in, and the day gently parks.

In the garden, the fireflies dress up like stars,
Flirt with the daisies, while arguing with cars.
Their sparkle is puzzling, a riddle so bright,
Illuminating secrets hidden deep in the night.

A hedgehog recites all the best bedtime tales,
While a rabbit contemplates turning to scales.
"Why not be a fish?" he shouts with great glee,
"When life's full of choices, why can't I just be?"

So pause in this moment, let laughter take wing,
As twilight holds secrets, we giggle and sing.
Though we may not discover, we giggle instead,
For each quirky conundrum, with joy we're well fed.

Uncharted Waters of the Mind

In the ocean of thought, I paddle alone,
With sea monsters lurking, they're grinning like stone.
I ask where the map is, the GPS fails,
Just me and my coffee, adrift on wild gales.

I dived for the treasure of wisdom so bright,
But all that I found was a sock in mid-flight.
The bubbles of brilliance, they swirl and they pop,
Leaving me wondering when genius will stop.

My brain's like a buffet, a feast on a whim,
A platter of nonsense, a buffet gone dim.
I forked over logic, it's lost in the haze,
Still searching for meaning in this foodie maze.

So, here's to the currents, both deep and absurd,
To thoughts that are silly, a fine flock of birds.
We sail down the rivers of hilarious dread,
In uncharted waters, where laughter is fed.

The Allure of the Unknown

The mystery beckons, a sign on the door,
Inviting me in, though I've never been poor.
I ponder the fate of the socks left to roam,
As they tap dance together, far far from home.

What happens to thoughts that go wandering back?
They might find a party, but could face a hack.
The allure of the unknown is swaying my mind,
Like jelly-filled donuts, so tempting, and blind.

With each tiny mystery, I nibble bit by bit,
Like secrets on tongues that are covered in grit.
The allure drives us forth, curious and brave,
While logic is napping, we're lost in the wave.

And here amidst shadows where riddles abound,
We chuckle at reasons that never were found.
In laughter we linger, exploring our fate,
The allure keeps us guessing - it's never too late.

The Melancholy of Forgotten Smiles

Once there was a smile, now it's lost in a drawer,
With dust on its laughter, and cobwebs for more.
It tries to escape, find a face to adorn,
But ends up in chilly company, forlorn.

The giggles and chuckles, like ghosts in the night,
Haunt hollowed-out faces, a comical fright.
Each grin hides a story, a twist and a turn,
Of how laughter was cherished, then left to just yearn.

In search of the smile, I wear mismatched socks,
Like badges of honor, I'll break all the clocks.
Trying to tick-tock my way to a grin,
I'll gather the chuckles, let the laughter begin.

So here's to the lost ones, the smiles we retrace,
Let's wear them like crowns in the silliest place.
For though they were forgotten, they'll always compile,
The melancholy treasures of our quirky style.

Tales from an Absent Tomorrow

Tomorrow's a ghost that won't show up in time,
It canceled its plans, oh, what a crime!
I waited with justice, a scale in my hand,
But ended up laughing, it didn't understand.

I texted my future, the message went lost,
It breezed by like winter, oh, what a cost!
Still, I pen little notes to my absent friend,
With doodles and hopes that our time will blend.

The secrets of 'later' are tangled like threads,
With socks in the dryer, and thoughts in the beds.
Yet every time I peek at what's just out of reach,
I chuckle at notions that time likes to teach.

So here's to tomorrow, that tricky old chap,
With riddles wrapped tightly in a colorful wrap.
I'll dance through the present, with dreams in tow,
For in tales from tomorrow, we'll find laughter's glow.

Threads of an Elusive Truth

In shadows cast, we weave a tale,
Spinning yarns that often fail.
A sock lost in the laundry's plight,
Is it magic, or just lost sight?

We chase our dreams, like cats in trees,
Mind the gaps, and dodge the bees.
But what's the truth behind the veil?
Perhaps it's just a funky snail.

Labyrinth of the Soul

In the maze where thoughts collide,
A squirrel's dance they can't abide.
We whirl around, with heads quite light,
Hoping to find a snack tonight.

Each corner turned, a new surprise,
Confusion wrapped in silly ties.
Do I laugh, or shed a tear?
Oh look, a llama – come here, dear!

Hidden Cravings

Beneath the masks we wear each day,
Lies a longing, come what may.
Chocolate bars and late-night snacks,
Satisfy when sanity cracks.

With each bite, we feel alive,
Pineapple on pizza, we strive.
In secret corners, we do meet,
Oh, the wonders of fast food grease!

The Dance of Dissonant Voices

In a choir of mismatched souls,
We sing our tunes, as chaos rolls.
One's off-key, the other's flat,
Yet somehow, we all find that.

The waltz of thoughts, a clumsy beat,
We trip and laugh on crazy feet.
A joke here, a pun right there,
Who knew confusion was such flair?

A Journey into the Unknown

We set sail on thoughts so wild,
As fate giggles, unbeguiled.
Each question marks a silly dance,
In riddles clad, we spin, we prance.

What's that lump in my sock drawer?
A lost time traveler's encore?
Or maybe just a dust bunny,
That eats up socks, oh how funny!

The fridge hums secrets, oh so loud,
Whispers of pickles in a crowd.
Mysteries swirl in yogurt cups,
And leftovers say, 'Fill me up!'

In shadows lurk the socks we miss,
Adventures in a laundry abyss.
With laughter, we embrace the strange,
Life's riddles, oh, how they arrange!

In the Realm of Uncertainty

Caught in the quirk of life's strange game,
We question our coffee's rightful name.
Is it brew or a potion of stealth?
Best sip it slow, preserve your health!

The cat stares deep into the void,
What secrets have you, little paranoid?
Do you plan a trip to outer space,
Or just plotting to steal my place?

We trip on thoughts that seem profound,
Yet often leave us sheerly confound.
In pursuit of wisdom, we find a joke,
Like searching for meaning in a poke.

As we juggle life's heavy load,
With laughs and quips upon our road.
Uncertain paths bring mirth and cheer,
I'll take the giggles over fear!

The Heart's Hidden Labyrinth

In chambers where absurd resides,
The heart leads forth on silly rides.
With a maze of doubts that twist and twine,
Love's compass points to a dither'd line.

With chocolates lost in the couch's grip,
I ponder love's bizarre manuscript.
Is it more swirls or tangled threads,
That keeps us wrapped in heart's true spreads?

Each tear a giggle, each sigh a cheer,
In love's absurd theater, we persevere.
With heart-shaped cookies promising fate,
We munch mystery pies while we wait.

In this labyrinth where shadows play,
We dance with quirks on this broadway.
So bring forth the snacks, let's toast the night,
In laughter's warmth, the heart feels right.

Traces of a Fading Light

As daylight dims, we hunt for clues,
Where left socks lie and rumors cruise.
In shadows, whispers swiftly dart,
What's lurking here? Is it just art?

The moon, a thief, laughs from above,
Is it snooping, or just in love?
It steals our bedspread, runs with glee,
What mischief does it plan, oh me?

In corners gathering years of dust,
What secrets linger, perfume, and crust?
Each fading light tells tales so bold,
Of coffee spills and yarns retold.

With wit as our lantern, we'll explore,
The chuckles hidden behind each door.
In laughter's grip, let shadows play,
For life's fading light leads us astray!

www.ingramcontent.com/pod-product-compliance
Lightning Source LLC
Chambersburg PA
CBHW051647160426
43209CB00004B/822